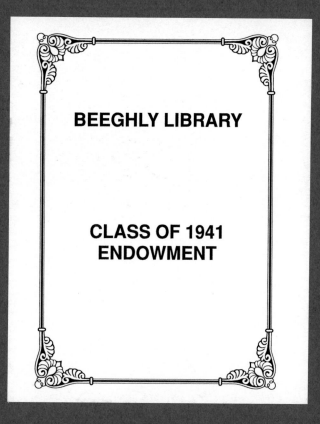

THE MAN WHO FLIES WITH BIRDS

CAROLE GARBUNY VOGEL AND YOSSI LESHEM

KAR-BEN
PUBLISHING

For Sally Nemzow Esakov,
with deep appreciation
for the many years of
friendship, laughter,
and insight
—CGV

In memory of the Israeli
Air Force pilots who lost
their lives in bird strikes
—YL

Captain Ronen Lev   Captain Yaron Vivente   Major Sephi Levine

ACKNOWLEDGMENTS

We acknowledge Dan Alon, director of the Israel Ornithology Center, who has made significant contributions to the field of ornithology. We also acknowledge Professor Yoram Yom-Tov, Tel Aviv University, Israel.

Dr. Leshem gratefully acknowledges the support from the following institutions: the Israeli Air Force; Society for Protection of Nature in Israel; Tel-Aviv University; International Center for the Study of Bird Migration, Latrun; Israel Ministry of Education; US-AID MERC; and German Federal Ministry for the Environment, Nature Conservation, and Nuclear Safety.

We appreciate the help of Dr. Carla J. Dove, program manager, Bird Strike Remains Identification Laboratory at the Smithsonian's National Museum of Natural History. Thanks to Robin Gordon, ASPNI, for her assistance. We are indebted to Jean Reynolds, our editor extraordinaire, and Joanna Sussman, the director of Kar-Ben Publishing, for believing in our book.

Last but most definitely not least, we thank our devoted spouses, Rivka Leshem and Mark A. Vogel, for their encouragement and enthusiastic support.

Kar-Ben Publishing
A division of Lerner Publishing Group, Inc.
241 First Avenue North
Minneapolis, MN 55401 U.S.A.

Website address: www.karben.com

Library of Congress Cataloging-in-Publication Data

Vogel, Carole Garbuny.
    The man who flies with birds / by Carole G. Vogel and Yossi Leshem.
      p. cm.
    Includes index.
    ISBN 978–0–8225–7643–3 (lib. bdg. : alk. paper)
    1. Birds—Migration—Israel—Juvenile literature. 2. Birds—Migration—Middle East—Juvenile literature. 3. Aircraft bird strikes—Israel—Juvenile literature.
4. Leshem, Yossi—Juvenile literature. I. Leshem, Yossi. II. Title.
    QL698.9.V63 2009
    598.0956—dc22   2008031198

Manufactured in the United States of America
1 2 3 4 5 6 – DP – 14 13 12 11 10 09

Long-legged buzzards typically hatch three chicks during a nesting season.

In the spring of 1972, a hiker in the Samarian Mountains northwest of Jerusalem might have been in for a big surprise. On a narrow ledge near the top of a steep, rocky cliff, a man crouched in a massive bird's nest. Dressed in shorts, sandals, and a rumpled T-shirt, he shared his perch with three frightened long-legged buzzard chicks. The baby birds huddled motionless in the bottom of the nest while their parents circled above, emitting loud, high-pitched screeches.

The man methodically plucked each bird from the nest, enclosed it in a sack, and placed the sack in a basket attached to a rope. A colleague at the top of the cliff pulled the rope, hoisting the basket up. The man soon followed, climbing up on a separate rope.

The man in the nest was Yossi Leshem, a young Israeli biologist, and this experience was about to determine the course of his life.

Long-legged buzzards return to the same area each spring but not to their old nests. Each year the buzzards build a new nest to avoid parasites in the old one.

   Working quickly, Yossi and his colleague weighed and measured the young buzzards. They tagged each of them with a small leg band and then gently stuffed the chicks back into their sacks. All the while, the adult birds continued to circle above, shrieking.
   Long-legged buzzards are raptors—birds of prey—and closely related to eagles and hawks. They hunt mice, voles, and other small rodents, as well as insects, birds, snakes, and lizards. Fully grown long-legged buzzards measure about 24 inches when standing and can have a wingspan of 60 inches. The one-month-old chicks that Yossi measured were nearly the size of their parents but had not yet grown all the feathers needed for flight.

BIRD BANDS Bird banding involves capturing a bird, tagging it, and then letting the bird go. The tag is usually an aluminum ring that is placed on the bird's leg. It contains the name of the banding agency and a unique number belonging to no other bird. The rings come in different sizes to ensure that each bird will have one that fits. They do not interfere with flight or other activities.

Most birds are caught in nets or other traps at banding stations along migration routes. Usually the bird is weighed, measured, and checked for parasites. Once they have been banded, individual birds can be identified by their tag number when they are recaptured later at the same place or at banding stations elsewhere. Banding stations exchange information about birds with other stations along migration routes. By tracking banded birds, researchers can learn about migration patterns, summer and winter homes, age, life span, birthrates, and health.

Most tags are rings, but some researchers will mark a large bird by attaching a colored plastic tag to its wing. These birds are identified by the tag color and the combination of letters and numbers written on it. Using binoculars, researchers in the field can read the tag without having to recapture the bird.

Putting identifying tags on birds is called bird banding in North America. In the Middle East and Europe, it is called bird ringing.

To release the young birds, Yossi picked up the sacks and returned to the cliff's edge, lowering himself carefully into the nest with the rope. After the chicks were safely nestled in their rightful places, Yossi lingered in the nest taking photographs. Perched on that narrow ledge with a bird's-eye view of the world, he made the decision to spend his life studying eagles and other raptors.

Mount Carmel has been a symbol of beauty since ancient times.

A BIRD'S EYE VIEW OF THE WORLD

Yossi's love for birds began when he was a little boy growing up in Israel. He was born in 1947 in Haifa, a city along the Mediterranean Sea. His father, Shmuel, showed no interest in birds or other wildlife. His mother, Klara, however, was a nature lover. She often took Yossi and his younger brother, Zvi, for hikes on nearby Mount Carmel. On these outings, Klara would ask the boys to sit quietly and listen to the sounds of the wind and wild creatures. Yossi spotted many different kinds of soaring birds and songbirds, but his mother could not identify them. Yossi jokes that she couldn't tell a bird from a donkey. Nonetheless, she did instill a love of nature in Yossi.

During Yossi's army service, he came across an injured desert eagle owl that had been hit by a car. He nursed the owl back to health and released it into the wild.

In 1964, when he was a teenager, Yossi explored Israel's Negev Desert with three of his friends. On one of these adventures, they met David Ben-Gurion, who had recently served as prime minister of Israel. For two hours, the boys hiked with Ben-Gurion, sharing their outlooks on the world. Then the famous leader invited the boys to his house, where his wife, Pola, served them tea and cake. This experience taught Yossi that he could share his ideas with powerful people.

From the time that Yossi was very young, he dreamed of flying with the birds. But poor eyesight kept him from his goal of becoming an air force pilot. Instead, Yossi served in the Israeli army for three years after high school. When he left the service, Yossi studied zoology and genetics at Hebrew University in Jerusalem.

Yossi never lost his fascination with birds. After graduation, he took a job with the Society for the Protection of Nature in Israel (SPNI), an organization committed to preserving Israel's wilderness areas and protecting wildlife. One of Yossi's coworkers at SPNI who was studying long-legged buzzards invited him to help with the banding. That was how Yossi ended up roosting in the buzzard's nest and getting the inspiration to be a raptor expert. He knew that some raptor populations in Israel were facing extinction. He wanted to work to save these birds.

BIRD STRIKES: A RESEARCH CHALLENGE

Yossi's military background and his interest in birds and flight all came together and led him to confront a terrible threat faced by military pilots: bird strikes. Bird strikes occur when a bird collides with a plane. Yossi first discovered this problem at the age of 36 when he went back to school to earn his Ph.D. He enrolled in an ornithology program at Tel Aviv University, and like all Ph.D. students, Yossi needed a research project. He decided to study the migration of raptors and the dangers these birds encounter.

Twice a year, 35 different species of raptors wing across Israel in mass migrations. Yossi wanted to know how many birds there were altogether and what routes they took. Bird-watchers with binoculars and telescopes had already counted 800,000 raptors from the ground during a single migration season. Yossi wondered if there could possibly be even more birds, ones that flew higher in the sky beyond the range of bird-watchers.

Charred remains of an Israeli F-16 hit by a golden eagle over the Judean Desert in 1988

A pilot suggested that Yossi count the birds from a plane. Although the idea was appealing to a man who loved to fly, Yossi could not afford to hire a plane. So he decided to ask the Israeli Air Force for the use of a small Cessna aircraft. This may seem like an unusual request, and indeed, it was. Who in the world approaches the military to ask to borrow a plane just to track birds? In a large country such as the United States, someone making such a request would not be taken seriously. But in a nation as small as Israel, more opportunities exist.

Early in 1983, Yossi obtained an appointment to present his request to an Israeli Air Force colonel. Yossi described his research proposal, but the colonel was skeptical. How could loaning Yossi a plane to study bird migration be of help to the military? By chance, the colonel that Yossi spoke with happened to be in charge of flight safety for the Israeli Air Force. During the visit, the colonel showed Yossi secret data. Between 1972 and 1982, the Israeli Air Force had suffered thousands of bird strikes. Thirty-three caused severe plane damage. In five of these collisions, the aircraft had been demolished. In one instance, the pilot had been killed. The financial cost was staggering—tens of millions of dollars in a single ten-year period.

When large migrating birds such as these storks fly in flocks, they pose an obvious risk to planes. But even one large bird, such as this honey buzzard flying solo, can bring down an aircraft.

This information stunned Yossi. He had thought a lot about bird migration, but he had never considered the impact of birds on aviation. Although troubled by the huge losses, he was also intrigued. Most of the strikes had happened during migration season when birds clogged the sky. The most damaging strikes involved large soaring birds—raptors, storks, and pelicans. With a clear understanding of bird migration, Yossi reasoned, the number of bird strikes could drop.

Yossi told the colonel that with enough funding for his project, he could map the migration routes of large birds. He could also give the military forecasts of when and where he expected the birds to appear. And finally, he promised up-to-the-minute reports of where birds actually were. With this data, pilots could avoid the paths of the birds. To drive home his point, Yossi predicted that during the first two weeks of May, a million honey buzzards would pass over Israel.

FOR 60 MILLION YEARS, BIRDS RULED THE SKY. They used the boundless space for hunting, for courtship, and as a highway for travel. Insects and bats shared the air but posed no threat—there was plenty of room for all. In 1903, however, brothers Orville and Wilbur Wright demonstrated their powered flying machine, and trouble soon followed. The first collision between a bird and plane occurred in 1905. Circling over an Ohio cornfield, Orville Wright chased a flock of birds and struck one. Orville and the plane escaped unhurt, but the bird died.

Seven years later, on April 3, 1912, Calbraith Perry Rodgers became the first human to meet his demise in a bird and aircraft encounter. Rodgers was flying along the California shore when a flock of gulls suddenly crossed his path. To avoid the birds, Rodgers nosed the plane down into a steep dive. He couldn't recover from the plunge, and the plane crashed into the surf.

Four months before his fatal crash, Calbraith Perry Rodgers became the first person to fly coast to coast across the United States. This feat required 70 stops and took 49 days. Rodgers was the grandson of Commodore Oliver Perry, a U.S. Navy officer who became a hero during the War of 1812.

The first bird to die in a collision with a plane was likely a red-winged blackbird.

Rodgers piloted the Vin Fiz Flyer, a plane built by the Wright brothers.

The colonel listened respectfully to Yossi's ideas, but Yossi left the meeting without a commitment for any kind of funding from the military. Several months later, in May, Yossi received an urgent message from the colonel: "Meet me at headquarters at eight o'clock tomorrow morning."

At the meeting, Yossi learned that on the previous day a honey buzzard had destroyed a Skyhawk, a five-million-dollar fighter plane. The pilot survived because the bird crashed through the windshield and struck the ejector handle. The bird not only launched the pilot, but it also launched Yossi's career. The air force decided to pay for his research.

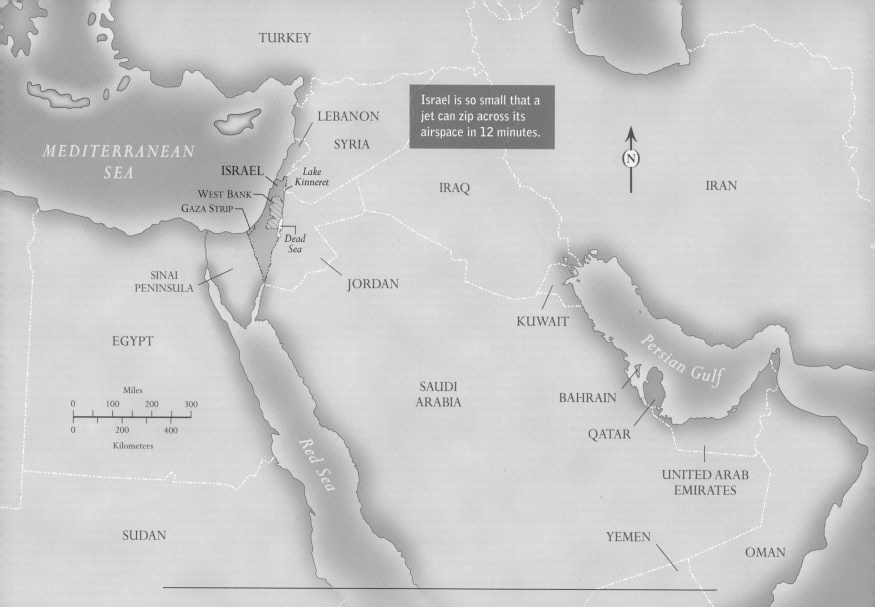

TURKEY

LEBANON

SYRIA

Israel is so small that a
jet can zip across its
airspace in 12 minutes.

MEDITERRANEAN
SEA

ISRAEL *Lake
Kinneret*

WEST BANK

GAZA STRIP

*Dead
Sea*

SINAI
PENINSULA

JORDAN

EGYPT

Miles

0   100   200   300

0   200   400

Kilometers

IRAQ

IRAN

N

KUWAIT

Persian Gulf

SAUDI
ARABIA

BAHRAIN

QATAR

UNITED ARAB
EMIRATES

Red Sea

SUDAN

YEMEN

OMAN

ACCIDENTS WAITING TO HAPPEN

Bird strikes are a concern worldwide, but the tiny nation of Israel in the Middle East
faces a more difficult challenge than other countries. Twice a year, 500 million birds
fly over Israel. They migrate between their winter feeding grounds in Africa and their
summer nesting areas in Europe and Asia.

Israel is slightly smaller than the state of New Jersey. Located at the junction of
Africa, Europe, and Asia, Israel is a bottleneck for migrating birds. From the ground,
the massive flocks of migrating birds are a wondrous sight, but in the air, they are a
pilot's worst nightmare. An eight-pound stork may not look dangerous. But if it collides
with a jet flying 500 knots per hour, it can bring down the aircraft as effectively as a
missile. With half a billion feathered creatures in the tight airspace over Israel, clashes
between birds and planes appeared to be unavoidable—until Yossi came along.

THE WORST LOSS OF HUMAN LIFE from a bird strike occurred in 1960 during a takeoff at Logan Airport in Boston, Massachusetts. An Eastern Airlines Elektra aircraft plowed through a flock of starlings six seconds after the wheels left the ground. Starlings were sucked into three of the four engines. The plane lost power, bounced back to the ground, and careened off the end of the runway. It crashed into Boston Harbor, killing 62 of the 72 persons aboard.

A SIMILAR DISASTER was averted on January 15, 2009, when geese were sucked into both engines of a US Airways jet taking off from New York City's LaGuardia Airport. The pilot landed the plane safely in the Hudson River and all aboard were rescued.

This painting shows white storks soaring over the city of Jerusalem.

Yossi knew that restricting the activities of Israeli Air Force planes during migration seasons was not an option. Tensions in the Middle East are high. Israel maintains a strong air force, as do most of its Arab neighbors. Since its birth as a nation in 1948, Israel has kept its military powerful to protect its borders.

Military pilots must train at high speeds and low altitudes. They face a greater risk of midair bird strikes than airline pilots who soar to high altitudes immediately after takeoff. During the 1960s and 1970s, the Israeli Air Force was losing more planes to birds than to hostile fire. In 1982, the year Israel totally withdrew from the neighboring Sinai Peninsula, the nation's problem with bird strikes worsened.

Israeli Air Force F-16s fly maneuvers over the Negev Desert in southern Israel.

Sinai is about three times bigger than Israel. Nearly all of it is desert—dry, rugged, and barren. In 1967, during the Six-Day War, Israel took control of Sinai from Egypt. Over the next twelve years, the Israeli Air Force used the huge airspace above Sinai to train pilots. Then the tiny nation signed a peace treaty with Egypt and agreed to a gradual pullout from Sinai in exchange for peace. In 1982, when the withdrawal was complete, the Israeli Air Force was confined to the much smaller airspace over Israel. During migration seasons, the pilots had to share their narrow patch of sky with millions of birds. Military officials feared that the number of bird strikes would soar.

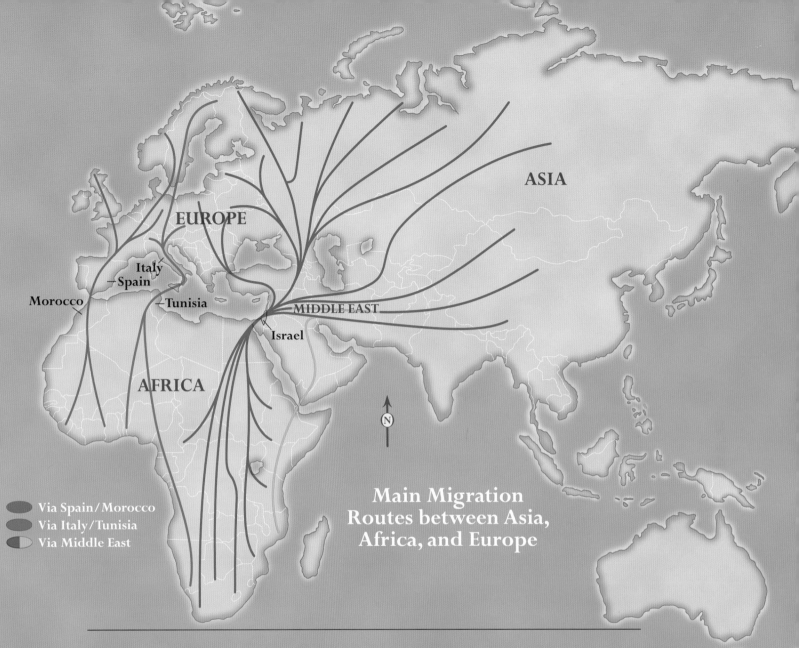

Main Migration Routes between Asia, Africa, and Europe

ASIA

EUROPE

Italy
Spain

Morocco

Tunisia

MIDDLE EAST

Israel

AFRICA

N

Via Spain/Morocco
Via Italy/Tunisia
Via Middle East

UNDERSTANDING MIGRATION

Yossi realized that the key to reducing bird strikes was to fully understand bird migration over Israel. In spring after migrating birds pass through the Middle East, they spread out across Europe and Asia, returning to nest in the place where they were hatched. In the nesting grounds, food is usually plentiful enough during growing season for adult birds to produce and raise a new generation. When the growing season ends, the food supply dwindles. The feathered travelers head back to their winter quarters in Africa. On the way, they once again pass through Israel.

Migrating birds share their winter homes with birds that live in the area year-round. Normally, during the winter months there is sufficient food to feed both the resident

MOST MIGRATING BIRDS JOURNEY IN A NORTH-SOUTH DIRECTION.

The Arctic tern holds the record for long-distance commuting. This seabird nests in the Arctic near the North Pole during summer in the Northern Hemisphere. Then, when it is autumn in the Northern Hemisphere, the Arctic tern moves southward as shown on the map, heading to the Antarctic coast near the South Pole, where it will soon be summer again. (When it is winter in the Northern Hemisphere, it is summer in the Southern Hemisphere and vice versa.) This bird of nearly endless summer makes a round trip of up to 26,000 miles each year. That is a longer distance than flying around the world at the equator.

and migrating birds. However, in the nesting season, the demand for food jumps. There is not enough food for all.

The migrating birds take wing again and return to their summer homes. They may fly over vast, sun-baked deserts, snowy mountain ranges, or immense stretches of water. They can encounter bitter-cold temperatures, fierce winds, and pelting rain or snow. To survive, birds must equip themselves with sufficient energy reserves to fly long distances without eating.

The timing of migration is a matter of life or death. It is controlled by cues from the environment and an internal clock that keeps birds in tune with the seasons. The sun plays a major role.

Geese can fly 3,700 miles on
their fat reserves.

In autumn there are fewer hours of sunlight and the sun does not rise as high in the
sky. The air grows colder. Birds must prepare for their odyssey before the food supply
shrinks. Prior to migration, a bird feels hungry all the time and goes on an eating
binge. Birds with the longest treks may nearly double their normal weight. Those
facing shorter journeys gain less. A bird's body changes the excess food into fat and
stores it under the skin, mainly in the chest area. The fat provides fuel that is so rich in
energy that some birds can remain airborne for more than 24 hours without a break.

A bird's internal clock triggers the eating marathon, but the length of day
determines the exact day of flight. With the onset of cold weather, insects disappear.
Therefore, the insect-eating birds, such as honey buzzards, become the first to
migrate. As sunlight diminishes and temperatures plummet, reptiles and amphibians
retreat underground or settle on lake or pond bottoms for the winter. With little to
eat, their predators leave next. When the tops of lakes and ponds freeze, fish become

unreachable, so fish-eating birds depart. The cold finally drives mammals into sheltered places, and mammal-eating birds take off.

The order is reversed in the spring. Mammal eaters return to the nesting places first, followed by amphibian eaters, reptile eaters, and then insect-munching birds. Arriving too early at the nesting areas can be fatal. If the weather is too cold and no food can be found, the birds will starve. Global warming is already impacting migration patterns. Some birds have changed the timing of their migrations. They arrive earlier in the nesting grounds in spring and leave later in the fall.

At the onset of migration, the tiny ruby-throated hummingbird weighs about as much as two pennies. Fat reserves make up almost half of its weight. Using this fat to power its flight, the hummingbird can fly 600 miles in 26 hours without stopping to "refuel."

Yossi, like other scientists, wondered how birds find their way between nesting and wintering grounds. Some kinds of young birds learn the route from their parents. Most make the long journey without parental help. How do they know where to go? What guides these birds over oceans where no landmarks exist?

Scientists have not unraveled the mystery of bird migration completely, but a few things have become clear. Birds have specialized senses, some of which are quite different from those of humans. Their senses can detect phenomena that humans cannot pick up.

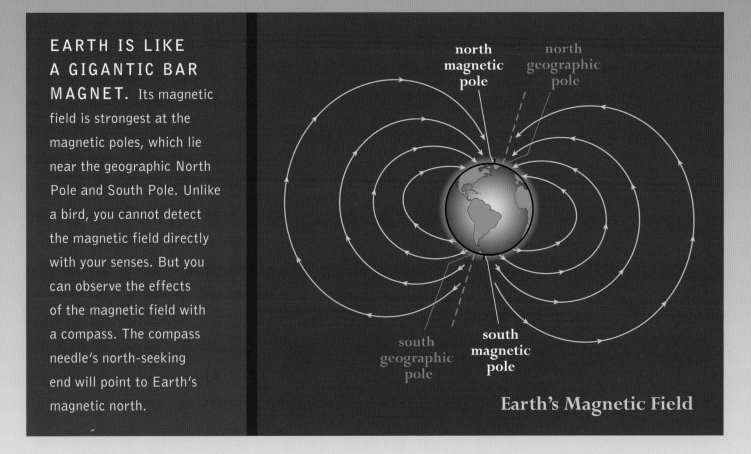

EARTH IS LIKE
A GIGANTIC BAR
MAGNET. Its magnetic field is strongest at the magnetic poles, which lie near the geographic North Pole and South Pole. Unlike a bird, you cannot detect the magnetic field directly with your senses. But you can observe the effects of the magnetic field with a compass. The compass needle's north-seeking end will point to Earth's magnetic north.

north magnetic pole

north geographic pole

south geographic pole

south magnetic pole

Earth's Magnetic Field

Birds seem to sense Earth's magnetic field and read it like a road map. The "map" tells them where they are and where they want to go. Their brains may contain magnetite, a form of iron that acts like a compass needle. (One end of a compass needle always points north.) This internal compass lets the birds know when to change direction. It is almost like having a built-in Global Positioning System (GPS).

Birds may also depend upon the landscape for guidance and follow rivers, coastlines, and mountain ranges. Odors might play a role. The scent of the air varies from place to place. Birds may have a sense of smell sharp enough to detect minute differences in these odors.

Nighttime fliers may orient themselves by the position of the setting sun and star patterns. In the Northern Hemisphere, the North Star is almost directly above the North Pole. It appears to stay in one spot while the Big Dipper and four other nearby constellations circle it. In the Southern Hemisphere, there is no "South Star" positioned over the South Pole. However, two stars in the Southern Cross constellation point toward the South Pole.

THE PHYSICS OF FLYING

In his studies, Yossi also learned the mechanics of bird flight. When a bird flies, its wings stir up the air directly above them, creating a tiny tornado. The swirling air creates a low-pressure zone over the wings. Below the wings, the zone of air has higher pressure. The higher pressure air pushes the bird upward. Fittingly, this push is called lift.

In some flocks, birds fly in V-shaped formation to take advantage of the lift produced by other birds. A bird flying behind the wing tips of another uses the swirling air to increase its own lift. All the birds in a V-shaped formation save energy except for the leader. Since the lead bird gets no benefit, the birds take turns being first.

Migrating birds fall into two groups: soaring birds and active fliers. Most small birds are active fliers. They power their flight by flapping their wings. Active fliers can cross massive bodies of water. When they do so, they fly night and day over the most direct route. The flight muscles of flapping birds generate a tremendous amount of heat

A stork's average flying speed is about **21** knots, but after leaving a thermal, it can glide at a rate of **32** to **43** knots.

Flying through cool night air helps birds lose heat. It reduces the chance of overheating. Over land, active fliers take off after sundown and roost before sunrise.

Sometimes active fliers catch a ride on winds blowing in the direction they are going. These tailwinds give the birds a rest and whisk them to their destination sooner. Strong headwinds (winds blowing in their faces) slow the birds' progress. In a headwind, the birds expend more energy and cannot rest. If they meet a storm at sea, the gales can blow them off course. The birds may become so fatigued from fighting fierce wind that they die.

Soaring birds are large with wide wingspans. They are too heavy to journey vast distances by just flapping their wings. They fly mainly by soaring (sailing upward on air currents) and gliding (descending slowly over a long distance). To boost their flight, the birds tap the energy of thermals, swirling bubbles of warm air that flow upward from the ground. Soaring birds treat thermals as elevators in the sky.

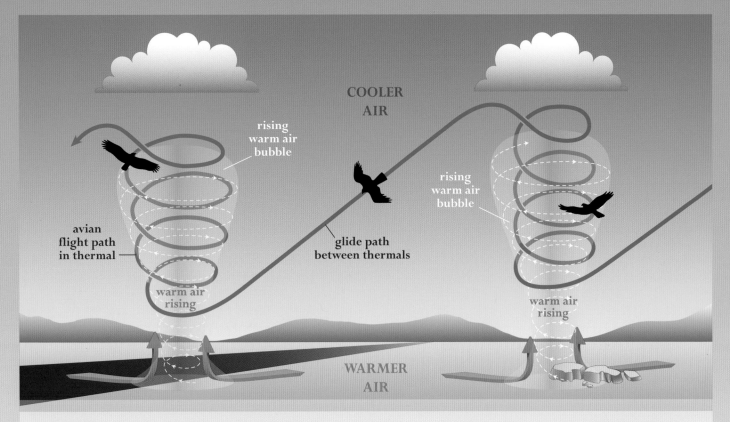

COOLER
AIR

rising
warm air
bubble

rising
warm air
bubble

avian
flight path
in thermal

glide path
between thermals

warm air
rising

warm air
rising

WARMER
AIR

Soaring birds spiral up a thermal and then glide to the next one. They can fly more than twice as fast inside a thermal than by flapping their wings.

THERMALS: ELEVATORS IN THE SKY

Solar energy powers thermals. When sunlight splashes the land, it heats the surface. In turn, the land warms the air above it. However, the sun does not heat the land evenly. Rocks, road surfaces, or patches of dry sand may heat up faster than the ground surrounding them. The air above these hot spots is warmer too.

A thermal forms when warm air is surrounded by slightly cooler air. The warm air expands and rises as a bubble. Gradually, the rising air cools and eventually cannot go any higher. The thermal breaks up. The cooled air spreads out and plummets back to the surface over the cooler terrain.

A thermal acts somewhat like a chimney. It draws in warm air near the bottom and channels it upward like smoke. The warm air spins as it rises, so birds hitchhiking on a thermal circle upward. When the thermal breaks up, the birds glide away. They gradually lose altitude until they find another thermal to whisk them skyward. In this way, soaring birds can travel large distances over land without flapping their wings.

Pelicans circling
upward inside
a thermal

Thermals begin to form after sunrise as the early heat of day chases away the chill
of night. Weak at first, thermals strengthen as the sun moves higher in the sky. Birds
begin to ride thermals between seven and nine in the morning. From late morning
to early afternoon, thermals are at their strongest. They can reach a height of nearly
a mile. In late afternoon, as the sun sinks lower in the sky, thermals fade. They
disappear completely after nightfall. So soaring birds migrate during the day and roost
at night.

Soaring birds can rise from the ground to the top of a thermal in about four to five
minutes. They save energy riding thermals even though they travel long distances to

Over a two-month period each spring and fall, 70,000 pelicans migrate through Israel.

Yossi was intrigued by the behavior of storks and raptors during migration. These birds travel in enormous flocks, sometimes numbering tens of thousands. On peak migration days, the lines formed by flocks extend up to 125 miles. Except for the leaders, the raptors and storks don't waste time and energy searching for the migration route or hunting for thermals. They simply follow the birds ahead of them, like marchers in one long parade.

Pelicans employ a slightly different strategy. Upon leaving a thermal, the pelicans break up into smaller groups, each flying in a V-formation. The groups set off in the same direction but spread out over a wide area. This makes it easier for the pelicans to find the next thermal. When a member of the flock spots one and starts to spin upward, the rest follow.

These helpful thermals do not develop over water. So, soaring birds cannot cross oceans and wide seas. Instead, the birds choose flight paths where good soaring conditions exist. They follow valleys, mountain ranges, and coastlines. The steep cliffs and rugged ridge lines in these landscapes are ideal for thermal formation. They also produce other rising air currents. When a breeze slams into a hill or cliff, the air must go somewhere, so it whooshes upward.

Most soaring birds migrating between Europe, Asia, and Africa take the shortest route around the Mediterranean Sea. They follow the Great Rift Valley. On bright, clear days, the valley's sun-kissed floor and slopes give birth to a seemingly endless string of thermals.

THE GREAT RIFT VALLEY is a 4,400-mile gash in Earth's rocky surface. It extends from Turkey in Europe to Mozambique in Africa. Bracketed by steep cliffs, the rift passes through Syria, Lebanon, and Israel in the Middle East. Continuing south, the rift is flooded by the Gulf of Aquaba and the Red Sea. In Africa the Great Rift Valley reappears and forms a wide, deep crack along the length of the eastern part of the continent. The rift runs from Ethiopia to Mozambique. A western branch stretches along the eastern border of Congo.

The Sea of Galilee in northeastern Israel is part of the Great Rift Valley.

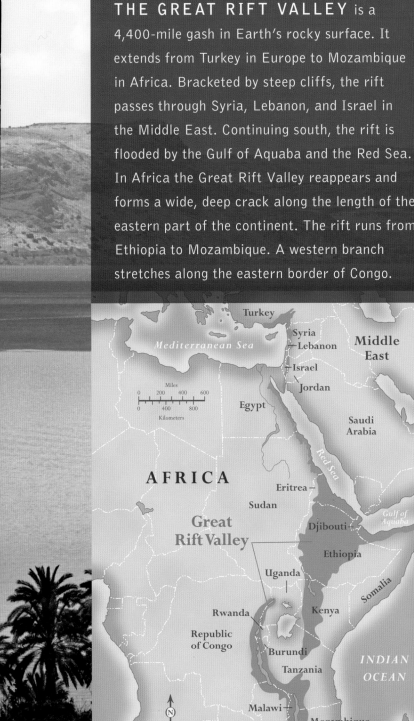

Turkey

Mediterranean Sea

Syria
Lebanon

Middle East

Israel

Jordan

Miles
0 200 400 600
0 400 800
Kilometers

Egypt

Saudi Arabia

Red Sea

AFRICA

Eritrea

Sudan

Great Rift Valley

Djibouti

Gulf of Aquaba

Ethiopia

Uganda

Somalia

Rwanda

Kenya

Republic of Congo

Burundi

INDIAN OCEAN

Tanzania

N

Malawi

Mozambique

Zambia

Bird-watching brings people together. An Arab landowner from Kfar-Quasem joined Israeli birders taking part in the migration survey for the Israeli Air Force.

A NETWORK OF WATCHERS

In ancient times, the inhabitants of Israel noticed that certain birds flew over their land at the same time every year. Bird migration is even mentioned in the Bible. Yet in the thousands of years that people knew about the birds, no one had counted them all or mapped their routes. There was no reason to go to all the trouble.

Since human lives were at stake, learning more about the birds was crucial. Yossi Leshem's challenge was to develop a plan to track the movements of the millions of birds. But this task was far too immense for one person. His research project ballooned. It became a joint study involving Yossi, the Israeli Air Force, SPNI, and Tel Aviv University. Hundreds of people took part, including more than 600 bird-watchers from 17 different countries. Yossi relied heavily on the guidance of his Ph.D. adviser, Professor Yoram Yom-Tov, and his other professors from the university.

The team began with observing autumn migrations. Yossi and his colleagues set up a network of 25 observation stations in northern Israel. He spaced the stations about one and a quarter to two and a half miles apart in a line spread across the country from the Mediterranean Sea to the Jordan River. Yossi placed the observation stations this close together to reduce the chance of missing any birds.

Each station was staffed by one to three bird-watchers who counted the winged travelers and recorded their direction of flight. Soaring birds were counted only as they left a thermal and began to glide. The stations communicated with one another by

Humans in biblical days likely saw the ancestors of these cranes. In Jeremiah 8:7, it was noted that "even the stork in the heavens knows her appointed times; the turtledove, swallow and crane observe the time of their coming."

radiophone to make sure that the same birds were not counted twice. The observers also noted how weather impacted the flight paths. Sudden changes in wind patterns could whisk the birds off course.

For spring migrations, Yossi repeated the procedure. This time he placed observation stations in southern Israel instead of the north, as the birds were entering Israel's southern border as they headed northward.

The bird-watchers provided Yossi with valuable data, but they could not give him everything he needed. They missed birds that flew high in the sky beyond the range of binoculars and telescopes. And after sunset, it was too dark for the bird-watchers to observe nighttime fliers.

The Israeli Air Force trained soldiers to track migrating birds with radar.

THE TOOLS OF TRACKING

Yossi used radar to gather more information. Radar can detect flocks riding air currents far above the ground and out of the view of bird-watchers. Since radar doesn't need sunlight to "see," radar can track birds day and night. It can also spot aircraft, clouds, and even insects.

Think of radar as a kind of flashlight. When a flashlight focuses a beam of visible light on an object, the light travels through the air, bounces back, and reaches your eyes. Radar sends out pulses of invisible radio waves or microwaves. When the invisible waves hit an object (such as a bird), the waves bounce back to the radar. The position of the object is shown as a blip—a dot—on a radar screen.

Radar measures the time it takes for bounced waves to return. The farther away an object is, the longer it takes the waves to travel back. Radar can identify the location of a bird flock, speed, and direction of flight. It can detect birds up to 65 miles away.

Initially, Yossi was delighted when the Israeli Air Force gave him the use of a Cessna airplane to monitor birds. However, when the Cessna neared a flock, the birds scattered.

Large birds reflect the invisible waves better than small birds, so radar can distinguish birds by size. But the Israeli radars cannot identify the kind of bird or count the number of individual birds in a flock. However, the radar operators can learn to estimate the number of birds in a flock by the size of the blip on the radar screen.

The radar Yossi used initially could not measure the altitude of flocks. To determine exactly how high the birds fly, Yossi needed to observe them from a plane. The airplane's instruments could give him precise data on speed, location, altitude, and direction.

The Israeli Air Force equipped Yossi with a single-engine Cessna aircraft. This light plane held a pilot and four passengers. Yossi was thrilled to be up in the air with the birds, but the birds did not feel the same. The engine noise frightened them, and they scattered whenever the plane came too close. The military pilot quickly learned to fly parallel to the birds at a distance of about 800 feet. The plane could not fly slowly enough to match the speed of the birds. This prevented Yossi from staying with a single flock as it traversed the country from one end to the other. Nevertheless, by tracking many different flocks, Yossi eventually worked out the three major migratory routes of the soaring birds.

Yossi was still not satisfied. Determined to accompany a single flock during its entire passage over Israel, he experimented with other types of aircraft. First, he tested a hang glider, but it couldn't stay aloft long enough. Next, he checked out an ultralight plane. It was unstable in strong winds and quite noisy. Finally, he tried a motorized glider—and it worked perfectly.

A motorized glider is a cross between a plane and a glider. Its motor allows it to take off and fly like a plane. When it is high in the air, the pilot can shut off the engine and ride the air currents like a bird. A motorized glider seats two people and can stay in the air for up to 11 hours.

The night before a glider flight, bird-watching teams on the ground would locate a stork, pelican, or raptor flock that had just roosted. The next morning when the birds resumed their journey, the glider would be flown into position to join them. With the

Yossi spent more than 1,400 hours observing birds from this motorized glider.

Raptors adjusted to the glider immediately. Storks took about an hour to become accustomed to it. Pelicans never got used to it. They were frightened by the sight of the flying machine. So when tracking pelicans, the glider stayed at least 325 feet away from them.

The glider traveled with the birds along their entire flight route in Israel. When the birds entered a thermal, the glider spiraled upward with them. At the thermal's crest, the glider gently drifted down until it caught the next updraft.

For Yossi the motorized glider was the ideal aircraft for studying a flock in flight. It enabled him to count every bird in the group. The instrument panel gave him the altitude, speed, and directional data that he needed to map the exact path of the birds.

There were difficulties though. Flying for hours with the birds tired the pilots. Yossi plied them with coffee, cookies, chocolate, and energy bars to keep them alert. The glider was not equipped with a toilet. There were special bags on board for the pilot and passenger to use if they needed to urinate. This only worked for men. Women were out of luck.

Soaring birds such as storks usually cruise at an altitude of about 3,000 feet. Strong thermals can lift them as high as 10,000 feet. Sometimes weather conditions can keep the birds as low as 300 feet.

The Israel Defense Forces provided Yossi with a drone, a small plane that flew without a pilot. Normally it was used for military surveillance, but Yossi used it to videotape flight paths of birds. Two people operated the drone by remote control from inside a truck. One person dealt with the actual flying of the aircraft. The other handled its complex camera system. This drone flew slowly and could stay aloft for five hours, providing enough time to follow a flock across the length of Israel.

The drone was flown about 5,000 feet above the migrating flocks. At that distance, none of the birds reacted to it, not even the easily frightened pelicans.

Yossi's project was the first time a drone from any nation was used for bird research. This drone could fly for five hours. Newer drones can stay aloft for two days.

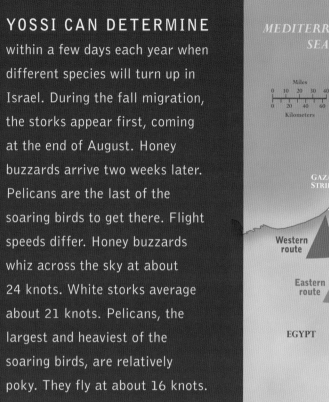

YOSSI CAN DETERMINE within a few days each year when different species will turn up in Israel. During the fall migration, the storks appear first, coming at the end of August. Honey buzzards arrive two weeks later. Pelicans are the last of the soaring birds to get there. Flight speeds differ. Honey buzzards whiz across the sky at about 24 knots. White storks average about 21 knots. Pelicans, the largest and heaviest of the soaring birds, are relatively poky. They fly at about 16 knots.

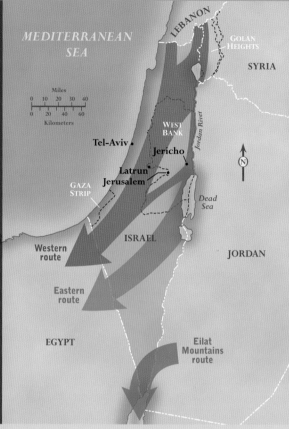

The drone sent the exact location of the birds' flight paths to a computer in the truck. From this data, the computer produced a map showing the migration route.

The drone had a drawback: it could not measure the altitude of the birds. If the drone operator lost sight of a flock, it could not be easily found again.

BIRD-PLAGUED ZONES

Yossi learned that there was no perfect tool for studying bird migration. However, when he combined the information collected from the bird-watching stations, radar, light aircraft, motorized glider, and drones, he ended up with startling results. The data revealed that four times as many birds migrate over Israel than previously thought!

The data also showed that soaring birds typically use one of three flyways—superhighways in the sky. The routes didn't vary much. But the height at which birds travel changes depending on the weather. Yossi's study confirmed the obvious. During the migration season, the flyways are so crowded with birds that the airspace becomes unsafe for planes.

To increase pilot awareness of birds, the Israeli Air Force introduced posters with the slogan, "Take Care—We Share the Air!" During migration season, pilots must pay strict attention to altitude when flying in bird-plagued zones. Most soaring birds migrate between ground level and 3,000 feet.

The solution to the bird strike problem was clear to Yossi: air traffic control. Birds cannot be instructed to change their flight behavior, so pilots must change theirs. Pilots needed to avoid the flight paths of birds. Yossi made two maps that marked bird-plagued zones. One map was for spring migration. The other was for autumn. Each map showed where and when each kind of soaring bird could be expected. Yossi also noted passage times—how long it took for a flock to cross Israel.

In 1984 the Israeli Air Force adopted Yossi's recommendation to ban planes from bird-plagued zones. Since the ban took effect, bird strikes in Israel have dropped by 76 percent, saving lives of pilots, as well as sparing birds and aircraft.

In 1999 officers from the air forces of Jordan, Turkey, Greece, the United States, and Israel attended a seminar on flight safety in the Middle East sponsored by Israel.

The same migrating flocks that jeopardize flight safety in Israeli skies endanger planes flying over Egypt, Jordan, and other nearby countries. Yossi realized that a regional warning system would be a good way to bring about cooperation between Israel and her neighbors. For example, during fall migration, Turkey could warn Jordan about birds entering Jordanian airspace. Jordan could warn the Israelis when the birds head their way. As a result, Israel is in the first stage of preparing a regional warning system with the air forces of Turkey and Jordan, as well as the U.S. Air Force.

The Israeli Air Force established a bird-watching center in Latrun. Known as the International Center for the Study of Bird Migration, it operates seven months a year, during the two migration seasons. As information from bird-watchers, radar units, and aircraft flows into the center, experts analyze it. They pinpoint the speed, altitude, and likely path of the flocks. They warn air force officials of immediate dangers to aircraft, advising them to call off flights or redirect them.

While the new regulations have greatly reduced collisions between birds and military aircraft, they have not eliminated them. After a bird strike, the Israeli Air Force launches the avian version of CSI (crime scene investigation). The military sends the bird remains to the Laboratory for Bird Remains Identification at Tel Aviv University.

The tiny structures of a feather, unique to each bird species, can easily be seen under an electron microscope.

CSI FOR BIRDS

Bird forensics began in the United States in 1960 with the deadly crash at Boston's Logan Airport. Investigators wanted to identify the flocking birds responsible for the disaster. They sent the bloody remains to the Division of Birds at the Smithsonian Institution in Washington, D.C. There, Roxie Laybourne used the institution's tremendous collection of dead, preserved birds to identify starlings as the culprit. Laybourne established the Feather Identification Lab at the Smithsonian and pioneered many of the current bird strike investigative methods.

After a bird strike involving a U.S. Air Force flight, the bird's remains are sent to the Feather Identification Lab. Researchers there use forensic techniques to identify the culprit. First, they wash the feathers to remove blood, grease, and dirt. Cleaning feathers may reveal their natural size, color, shape, and markings. The researchers can then identify the bird by matching whole feathers to bird specimens in their collection.

Sometimes only blood, tissue fragments and maybe bits of feathers are all that remain of the bird. In these cases, the "bird detectives" turn to DNA analysis. They

Yossi's colleague, Judy Shamoun-Baranes, heads the Laboratory for Bird Remains Identification in Israel. She worked with the Royal Netherlands Air Force to develop the bird remains identification software.

compare DNA samples from the birds with a database of DNA from nearly every bird species in the United States and Canada.

If the DNA is too damaged to use, the researchers examine feather bits under a microscope. They focus on barbules, tiny structures in the feather's "fluffy area." These structures show what large group the bird fits into, such as hawk or perching bird. To narrow down the culprit to the exact species, the researchers must look at still other clues. From the feather bits, they try to determine the feather's texture, color, and any other identifying properties. Researchers consider the location, date, time of strike, and time of year to figure out what species the likely suspects are.

Israel's Laboratory for Bird Remains Identification uses many of the techniques developed by the Smithsonian. However, the Middle East and North America have different bird populations. The Israelis needed a way to identify their own bird species. Together with researchers from Holland, Israeli scientists developed a computer program to do the job. It provides identifying features for 200 common birds from Europe and the Middle East.

Before Yossi Leshem came on the scene, the Israeli Air Force had already begun a flight safety program. The air force was using fireworks and recordings of birds in distress to scare birds away from runways. The managers of Tel Aviv's Ben-Gurion Airport tried using trained falcons to scare other birds away from their runways. Unfortunately, it did not work well enough.

SAFETY IN THE SKIES

Most bird strikes occur during takeoff and landing. The large open spaces surrounding airport runways attract birds. They especially like vast expanses of short, closely mowed grass where they can easily catch insects and worms. Feathered fliers do not understand the danger of airplanes, and airport boundaries mean nothing to them.

Airport operators realize that they must take measures to safeguard the runways. At many facilities, the administrators manage the vegetation to make it less appealing. They remove trees to eliminate the nightly roosting places for flocking birds. They permit the grass to grow longer so birds cannot find food as easily. The long grass also makes it harder for the birds to detect their own predators. At some airports, harassment techniques such as trained falcons, fireworks, noise cannons, bright lights, and border collies are used to chase away birds.

Airplane manufacturers are also working on the problem. They have designed planes to better withstand bird strikes.

Collisions above 500 feet typically involve flocks of birds. In the skies over Canada and the United States, gulls, geese, ducks, hawks, vultures, pigeons, doves, and starlings cause the most midair collisions.

In 2006 about 7,000 bird strikes were reported for civilian aircraft in the United States. That same year, the U.S. Air Force logged more than 5,000. These numbers

Land-bound animals can cause problems at remote airports. Pilots landing in the Alaskan wilderness need to watch for moose on the tarmac. In some parts of Africa, zebra and other large mammals can wander onto landing strips.

look frightening, but in nearly all the strikes, the people aboard were unharmed. In the United States, far more people die in highway accidents each month than have died altogether in birds strikes since the invention of the airplane.

In 85 percent of the collisions, the aircraft showed little or no damage. For the remaining 15 percent, the destruction ranged from mangled wings to splintered engines to completely wrecked planes. The amount of damage caused by a bird depends upon its weight, where it strikes, and the speed of the plane. The heavier the bird and the faster the plane, the greater the impact will be. A collision with a flock of birds can be particularly destructive because of the many points of impact. In the United States, the total cost of damage from bird strikes exceeds more than half a billion dollars a year. It is passed along to airline passengers in higher fares and to taxpayers as part of the military budget.

LEFT: Yum! This barn owl is bringing a dead vole to its nest as a midnight treat for its young. ABOVE: The kestrel feeds its chicks the same kind of "snack," but it doesn't compete with the owl. Kestrels find prey in daylight, and owls hunt in the cover of darkness.

BIRDS ON RODENT PATROL

Thanks to Yossi's work, the pilots and their passengers are safer in the skies over Israel. The birds are safer as well, although they still face grave dangers on the ground. One of their biggest threats stems from the pesticides used to kill rodents. Worldwide, mice, rats, and voles destroy 35 percent of the crops planted. To eradicate them, farmers may spray their fields with pesticides—poisons. The pesticides pollute the soil and water. When rodents eat sprayed crops, toxins build up in their tissues. Poisoned rodents either die or move so slowly that birds of prey can easily pluck them off the ground. The poisons within the rodents then collect inside the bodies of the birds, slowly killing them.

To save the birds and the environment, Yossi wanted to reduce pesticide usage. And he came up with the perfect solution: natural pest control. Barn owls hunt rodents at night. Kestrels (small hawks) hunt them during the day. Together, they can provide

JORDANIAN AND PALESTINIAN FARMERS

suffered from the same rodent trouble as Israel. Would the Arab farmers be interested in Israel's solution? In 2002 Yossi and the Israeli growers invited their Jordanian and Palestinian neighbors to a conference on barn owls and rodent control. In Arab culture, owls are a sign of bad luck. No one accepted. The next year, the Israelis sponsored a conference on organic farming. This time some of the Jordanian and Palestinian farmers attended. During the program, the Israelis demonstrated the usefulness of barn owls. It was so convincing, that the Arab growers decided to give natural predators a chance. Within six years, 80 nesting boxes had been placed in Palestinian fields and 100 in Jordanian croplands.

LEFT: Yossi's counterpart in Jordan is a retired army general, Mansour Abu Rashid. General Rashid heads the Amman Center for Peace and Development, an important conservation group in Jordan. Once a warrior, the general now battles to save the environment. BELOW: General Rashid (FRONT ROW FAR LEFT) attended the signing of a historic peace treaty between Israel and Jordan, which he helped to negotiate.

farmers with round-the-clock rodent patrol. The birds are most effective when they have young chicks to feed. One family of barn owls can devour 2,000 rodents in a year. A kestrel pair with young can snare 15 voles a day.

In 1983 Yossi began an experiment. Working with Kibbutz Sde Eliyahu, a farming community in northern Israel, he swapped pesticides for natural predators. To attract barn owls, Yossi and the farmers placed nesting boxes in the fields before the nesting season. It took nearly 10 years, but Yossi proved his point. Where barn owls flourished, rodent populations plummeted. The idea spread to other Israeli farmers. By 2008 nearly 1,500 nesting boxes had been placed in fields and pesticide use dropped.

LEFT: More than 25,000 cormorants spend the winter in Israel. These voracious fish eaters plague fish growers when they raid fish ponds. ABOVE: It took this white stork more than 10 minutes to swallow a black *Coluber* snake.

SEEKING A BALANCE

Despite the success with natural pest control, making the environment and wildlife a priority for Israelis is a struggle. For the first 50 years of Israel's existence, the national government focused more on planting forests and developing farmlands than trying to preserve the wilderness. Most of the natural wetlands were drained. "Nature conservation is a luxury we cannot afford," was the refrain. Caught up in border disputes and threats to its very existence, Israel's struggle to survive was and is its chief priority.

The lack of natural wetlands triggered an unintended consequence for migrating soaring birds. Their bodies cannot store enough fat for a complete journey, so the birds hunt for food along the way. This often brings the birds into conflict with humans.

In spring, migrating birds cross Africa's immense Sahara before reaching Israel. This harsh, parched desert provides no food or water for most birds. As a result, some birds arrive ravenous in Israel. Since most of the natural wetlands are gone, pelicans and other hungry waterbirds seek fish farms. The birds frustrated fish growers by gobbling up the carp, tilapia, and other fish raised as cash crops in artificial holding tanks. To safeguard the fish, the fish growers frighten the birds. They set off noise cannons and fireworks and use other scare tactics.

The feathered poachers are not allowed to starve. Some hard-won victories have been achieved in nature conservation in Israel, including the protection and restoration

A flock of 2,000 white pelicans can guzzle down nearly two and a half tons of fish in one meal.

of several important areas to birds. The birds can find fish in Lake Kinneret. Or they can dine at Hula Lake, a lake deliberately stocked with fish for the birds.

About 30,000 cranes winter in the Hula Valley in northern Israel. They infuriate farmers when they forage in peanut and chickpea fields, eating everything in sight. Yossi's SPNI colleague Dan Alon found a solution. He established feeding stations for cranes where they are fed corn directly. The feeding stations attract bird lovers too. "Blinds" have been erected so people can observe birds without being seen. Each year, 250,000 visitors flock to the stations to watch the magnificent birds.

Nevertheless, the environment faces ongoing threats from farmers who want to cultivate more land and developers determined to construct new roads and new buildings. Unless concerned citizens can prove that preserving the wilderness has value, they will always battle against "progress."

LEFT: Five pairs of storks nest in this castle tower in Germany. ABOVE: Researchers outfitted a stork with a transmitter. They painted patches of blue and orange on the bird's wings so bird-watchers in the field can identify it.

A shared concern about storks connected Yossi with German scientists. During the 1950s, storks nearly vanished from West Germany, Denmark, and many other Western European countries. Lack of food for the storks was to blame. Pesticide usage and other modern farming practices reduced the number of small animals hunted by the birds. In addition, as cities and towns expanded and farmers drained wetlands, the habitats of the storks' prey vanished.

Storks construct untidy nests atop towers, chimneys, high rooftops, and utility poles, as well as in tall trees or on steep cliffs. Patched together from sticks and twigs and lined with grass and other soft materials, the bulky nests can grow to enormous proportions—

STORKS—THE MYTH AND THE REALITY

Have you ever heard the myth that storks bring babies? It likely began in Germany, where storks are considered a sign of good fortune. People encourage them to nest on their rooftops. Unfortunately, the fondness for storks is not shared worldwide. The European Union passed laws to protect storks in Germany and other member countries of this economic and political unit. But they could not protect storks elsewhere. Each year hunters along their migration routes in the Middle East and Africa kill storks for sport or food.

This stork managed to fly from Africa to Israel with a hunting spear lodged in its body.

more than seven feet wide and almost ten feet deep. Storks return to their nests year after year, and some nests have been used each nesting season for hundreds of years.

Yossi teamed up with Professor Peter Berthold, a German bird expert, and several other researchers. Their goal was to track the global movement of storks. They strapped small satellite transmitters onto the backs of 120 storks. The transmitters are light enough that they don't hinder flight. Yet they are powerful enough to send a radio signal into space where it is picked up by a French satellite, Argos. The satellite relays the signal to a ground station in France. From there, a computer transmits the data via the Internet to computers in the bird center in Latrun. Researchers use the information from the signal to identify the bird's location.

The transmitters make it possible to track birds as they migrate from their nests in Europe, pass through Israel, and eventually arrive at their winter homes in Africa. By pinpointing where the birds stop to eat, drink, and rest, the researchers identified the stopover sites that are the most important to protect.

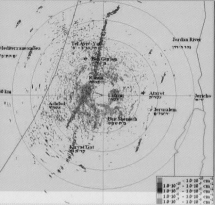

ABOVE: This is what 36,000 lesser spotted eagles look like on a radar screen. LEFT: The bird center at Latrun posts satellite tracking information at the Migrating Birds Know No Boundaries website: www .birds.org.il/. Students accessing the site can follow the progress of more than 100 storks, cranes, pelicans, and raptors outfitted with transmitters.

BIRDS HAVE NO BOUNDARIES

Yossi has logged more than 1,400 hours flying with storks and other migrating birds. Altogether, this adds up to flights on 272 different days. Spending so much time in the air made Yossi acutely aware that birds have no boundaries. Unlike people, they don't divide the land into national territories. Birds move freely over one large landscape, under one big sky. When the birds cross Israel's border and into the airspace of another nation, Yossi cannot follow. It is illegal to fly in the airspace of another nation without prior approval.

Migrating birds do not belong to one country. They are part of the natural world of all nations. Yossi wondered if a shared concern about birds could be used to connect people of different nationalities. Peace has to start somewhere, he reasoned, why not with birds?

Yossi contacted his Palestinian and Jordanian counterparts to get their input. Under the name Migrating Birds Know No Boundaries, Yossi's idea evolved into a joint research and educational program involving students in Jewish-Israeli, Arab-Israeli, Palestinian, and Jordanian schools. The program combines classroom studies, field observations, and satellite tracking of individual birds. Each tracked bird is given a Jewish, Christian, or Muslim name such as Tal, Lucas, or Fatima.

This radar station at the International Center for the Study of
Bird Migration is one of four radar systems in Israel dedicated
to monitoring birds. During migration seasons, the stations issue
bird warnings the way weather stations give weather forecasts.

One of Yossi's chief goals is to build public awareness about birds and nature
conservation. In 1995 SPNI and Tel Aviv University established the International
Center for the Study of Bird Migration in Latrun. Located halfway between Tel Aviv
and Jerusalem, Latrun is a memorial site for Israel's slain soldiers who served in the
tank corps. Yossi chose the location for the bird center because it is located in the
middle of the western bird migration route for soaring birds. And he hoped to share
his excitement about birds with some of the 400,000 tourists who visit the Latrun
memorial each year. The center became the hub for bird research and education in
Israel, with Yossi as its director. It houses a radar installation that supplies data to the
Bird Watching Center of the Israeli Air Force.

PEACE—ONE BIRD-WATCHER AT A TIME

For one brief period, Yossi glimpsed the possibility of achieving peace one bird at a time. From 1998 to 2000, he brought together students from Jewish-Israeli, Arab-Israeli, and Palestinian schools for a day of bird-watching. He divided them into teams of three, one student from each school. Cooperation among the students was achieved bird by bird as the children worked together to locate and identify birds. In 2000 he had his greatest success when 5,000 students came together at Latrun. Later that year, unrest in the region forced Yossi to suspend the integration of students. But he continues to work with his Palestinian and Jordanian partners in the program.

RIGHT: For more than 35 years, Yossi and his colleagues have been working with children and adults from the world over who come to Israel to look at the birds. BELOW: Imad Atrash, director of the Palestine Wildlife Society, is with a group of Palestinian students at the bird observatory in Jericho.

The most exciting time comes when the birds migrate through the Middle East. A bird may enter Syria in the morning and fly over Jordan, the West Bank, Israel, Gaza, and land in Sinai in the afternoon. As the students follow "their" birds online, they discover that some children outside their nation's borders share the same passion for the same birds.

Yossi hopes that someday when tensions lessen in the Middle East, Jewish and Arab students along the migration routes will be able to communicate directly with one another via the Internet. They could exchange bird information with children who live in nations that are traditional enemies of their own country.

Migrating Birds Know No Boundaries was such a success that it expanded to include schools in Europe and North America. By 2007 about 350 Israeli schools (Jewish and Arab), 30 Palestinian, 30 Jordanian, 5 Russian, and 5 U.S. schools were participating in the program. More schools were expressing interest. Still Yossi wasn't satisfied. He wanted to reach all the students in every Israeli school, and their parents, grandparents, aunts, uncles, cousins, and their entire extended families. In short, he wanted to make all Israelis take notice of the birds.

FOR 13 YEARS, schoolchildren participating in Migrating Birds Know No Boundaries used the Internet to track the movements of a white stork named Princess. They mapped her migration routes and recorded her arrival dates at places along the way. The green line on the map at right shows Princess's journey from Europe to Africa in autumn 1994. The red line indicates her return pathway in spring 1995. Every spring she nested with her mate in Germany. In the fall, Princess flew to her winter home in Africa. In 2000 her mate died. The next year, when Princess returned to Germany, she reclaimed her old nest and took a new mate, Jonas. Jonas had spent his winters in Spain, and he continued to do so. Princess always took her familiar path to Africa. But each summer, Princess and Jonas nested together and raised a family until she died in 2006.

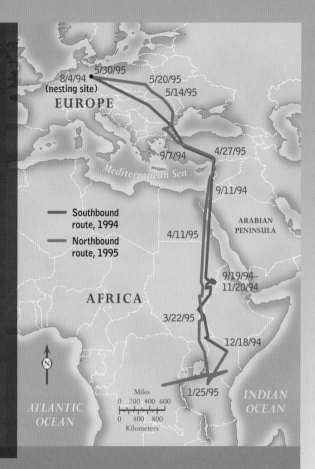

Princess flying with the transmitter strapped to her back.

This poster shows the ten nominees for the national bird of Israel. Each bird is identified by its English, scientific, and Hebrew names.

ISRAEL SELECTS A NATIONAL BIRD

How do you make a million people care about birds? How do you get a nation to pay attention to its natural environment? Yossi and his SPNI colleague Dan Alon came up with an idea to increase awareness of birds and nature among Israelis.

In May 2008, Israel celebrated the 60th anniversary of its birth. To mark the occasion, Yossi and Dan suggested that Israeli citizens select a national bird. After all, the United States has its bald eagle; Canada, its common loon; Great Britain, its robin; and Japan, its crane. Choosing a bird, however, that reflected Israel's national character was no easy chore. Candidates needed to be colorful birds that made pleasant sounds and nested in Israel. Being mentioned in the Bible and other important Jewish texts was an advantage.

Bird experts selected 50 birds as possible candidates. A convention of about 1,000 bird lovers narrowed the field down to 10. Israel is a democracy, so it was fitting that the final choice of a national bird was made in a national election. Prior to voting, SPNI

The winning bird was the hoopoe. It is a beautiful bird with a long beak and an orange and black crown. The hoopoe takes excellent care of its chicks and defends itself with creative tactics if attacked.

posted pictures and descriptions of the feathered contenders on its website. Each bird was represented by a "political party" whose members campaigned for their candidate. Newspapers and television stations reported on the election activities. Ballot boxes were placed on every military base in Israel, and all the soldiers voted. The public voted online or by phone.

The choice of a national bird was too important to be left to adults only. The children in all 4,000 public schools in Israel and all 9,500 kindergartens were given the chance to vote too. During the month before the election, the students learned about each species of bird and the threats to its environment.

More than 350,000 people cast their votes. Israel's president, Shimon Peres, announced the winner. The hoopoe became the national bird of Israel. This election proved to be an effective lesson in birding and democracy.

To protect his young from the extreme summer heat, the male stork placed wet straw in the nest to cool the chicks.

A STORK REALITY SHOW

Yossi and his colleagues found other ways to focus the public's attention on birds. They installed birdcams at nesting sites in Israel. Birdcams are digital cameras connected to the Internet. They provide live, close-up images of birds during courtship, mating, egg laying, egg tending, and rearing of young. During nesting season, live broadcasts of nesting kestrels and other birds can be viewed at the Latrun bird center's website.

One spring a pair of white storks captured the hearts of Israeli bird-watchers. These birds normally nest in parts of Europe and Asia where summers are cooler than in Israel, where summer temperatures soar so high you can fry an egg on the sidewalk. Bird lovers were puzzled when the storks built a nest at Kibbutz Tirat Zvi, a farming community near the Jordan River. Didn't the "bird brains" know the intense heat could harm their eggs?

Researchers mounted a birdcam near the nest so students and other bird-watchers could monitor the pair online. The storks successfully hatched two eggs, and the nest became a sensation. The birdcam site generated 165,000 hits.

At summer's end, the stork chicks and their mother joined a flock of migrating storks and flew to Africa for the winter. The male stork remained year-round at the nesting site.

As spring changed to summer, temperatures sizzled above 120°F. Worried bird-watchers fretted that the baby storks would soon become fried chicks. To everyone's surprise, the parents knew how to air-condition the nest. The mother spread her wings and placed her back to the sun, shading the babies. The father brought the chicks water to drink in his bill, and he sprinkled water on them to cool them off. Every 15 minutes, he collected straw in his beak, dipped it in a puddle, and nestled it next to his offspring.

No bird expert before had witnessed a bird cooling its young with wet straw. But 70 years earlier, the original settlers of the kibbutz had employed a similar technique. They placed a netting of wet straw over their open windows to cool off their homes.

Ecotourism is the key to protecting Israel's environment.

ECOLOGICAL TOURISM:
A WINNING PROPOSITION

Bird-watching is big business. About 100 million people worldwide are bird-watchers. The most dedicated ones—known as birders—tend to travel to faraway places in pursuit of new species of birds. Could these bird-watchers be the key to nature conservation in Israel? About 280 species of birds migrate over Israel, and about 250 species live in Israel for at least part of each year. Israel is a birder's paradise. It is also a delight for nature photographers and painters of wildlife and landscapes.

Ecotourism—ecological tourism—appeals to travelers who want to visit natural settings while doing minimal harm to the environment. The potential for Israel and neighboring countries is enormous. Ecotourists will pay for a place to stay, food to eat, transportation, and guided tours. In doing so, they will prove that protecting wildlife can also help the people nearby by creating jobs for them.

Birders from all over the world visit Israel and nearby countries to see migrating birds such as these lesser flamingos in Eilat salt ponds in southern Israel.

To enrich the experience of birders and other nature enthusiasts, Yossi and his colleagues set up 10 bird-watching centers in Israel. The centers are located in hot spots—stopover sites that attract multitudes of birds. At each site, researchers and guides provide information and assist in bird identification. Palestinian and Jordanian conservation organizations each established three similar hubs. When peace comes to the Middle East, Yossi hopes that these 16 centers will work together to boost ecotourism in the region.

LEFT: Stuffed dead birds—usually raptors and colorful songbirds—are sold as souvenirs or decorations. RIGHT: Dead warblers hang from the belt of a hunter who planned to eat them for dinner.

SAVING THE BIRDS OF THE WORLD

In the 1980s, Yossi Leshem's dreams took flight as he helped the Israeli Air Force discover ways to reduce bird strikes. What began as an effort to improve flight safety for people also benefited birds. He realized that winged migrants face much greater dangers on the ground than in the air. Yossi worked hard to make birds safer in Israel, but he realized that birds need protection wherever they fly. Safeguarding birds globally became his new goal.

The idea that birds have a right to exist and should be protected is uncommon in most Mediterranean countries, the Mideast, and Africa. Except for Israel, bird hunters far outnumber nature lovers along migration routes. Each year, hunters in the Mediterranean kill as many as one migrating bird in ten. This adds up to tens of millions of birds. Shooting birds is a popular sport—the bigger the bird the better. Laws controlling hunting are largely ignored. Some slaughtered birds are eaten, but most are shot for fun.

In all Mediterranean countries, songbirds are killed for food even when other food is plentiful. One method of trapping involves placing sticks smeared with glue alongside bushes or trees. When songbirds perch on the gooey sticks, they get stuck. Hunters also

Bee-eaters are considered a culinary treat in Mediterranean countries.

string nylon fishing nets between trees to snag birds. The hunters play recorded bird calls to lure the birds to the nets. The nets are nearly invisible, and the unwitting birds become entangled in them.

Trappers kill all the birds and discard the less tasty ones. Prized as a delicacy, the remaining songbirds are plucked and then pickled or roasted. Diners swallow them whole and spit out the beaks. A single meal consists of 12 or more birds. In Cyprus and Malta, songbird carnage is especially widespread.

Most birds escape hunters, but they still face other hazards during migration. Airplanes, power lines, and pesticide poisoning present immediate dangers. So do the destruction of stopover sites, nesting sites, and wintering grounds. Climate change due to global warming will create new challenges in the future.

Birds will be electrocuted if they touch two power lines at once. Large birds, such as raptors and storks, are at high risk because they can easily span the distance between two wires. This is a serious problem because birds view electrical poles as safe places to perch.

In food-poor regions in Africa, the ability to kill a bird may make the difference between eating a meal or going hungry. Solving the famine crisis will ease the hunting pressure on birds. Sustainable hunting is the goal.

Yossi dreams big, and his biggest dream is to have the Great Rift Valley declared a World Heritage Site. The valley—the longest geological phenomenon on Earth—spans 22 nations. It serves as the main flyway between Africa and Europe and Asia. Traversed by half a billion birds in the spring and fall, it is one of the most important migratory paths in the world. To guarantee the birds' survival, the natural setting of the Great Rift Valley must be protected forever. Yossi thinks ecotourism will play a critical role. So will promoting good hunting and farming practices. To reduce the risk of bird electrocution, power companies can install "bird friendly" devices on their equipment.

Ethnic, cultural, and religious differences separate the countries straddling the Great Rift Valley. Can the nations look past their differences and work together to safeguard the birds?

Since ancient times, the dove has been a sign of peace. Thanks to the work of Yossi and his colleagues, will the next winged messenger of peace be a stork, a barn owl, or even a honey buzzard that brings nations together?

Dr. Yossi Leshem's extensive knowledge about birds and bird strikes provided the basis of this book. Advanced readers can read more about his work in his book for adults, coauthored with Ofer Bahat, *Flying with the Birds* (Israel: Yedioth Ahronoth Books, 2009).

If a fictional character could be a kindred spirit, then Yossi's would be Juan, the young protagonist of *Songs of the Swallows*, by Leo Politi (New York: Scribner, 1949). This Caldecott Medal–winning book immortalizes the annual return of the swallows to San Juan Capistrano Mission and the boy who loved them.

Further Reading

Hoose, Phillip. *The Race to Save the Lord God Bird*. New York: Melanie Kroupa Books, 2004.

Lerner, Carol. *On the Wing: American Birds in Migration*. New York: HarperCollins, 2001.

Markle, Sandra. *Outside and Inside Birds*. New York: Bradbury Press, 1994.

Salmansohnm, Pete, and Stephen W. Kress. *Saving Birds: Heroes Around the World*. Gardiner, ME: Tilbury House, 2003.

Wechsler, Doug. *Bizarre Birds*. Honesdale, PA: Boyd's Mill Press, 1999.

Websites

Audubon New York
http://ny.audubon.org/
missionmigration.html
Play the Mission Migration game
to learn how the choices you
make at home, school, and in your
neighborhood impact migrating
birds.

Migrating Birds Know No Boundaries
http://www.birds.org.il/
To learn more about the work of
Yossi Leshem and his colleagues
at the International Center for the
Study of Bird Migration, visit their
website.

Project Get Out and Walk
http://www.ejection-history.org.uk/
Birds/birdstrikes.htm
This website provides a
comprehensive worldwide listing of
known bird strikes. It provides the
date, nation, type of aircraft, bird
species involved (when known), and
description of each strike.

Smithsonian National Zoological Park
http://nationalzoo.si.edu/Animals/
Birds/Facts/
In addition to outlining the park's
activities, this website provides fact
sheets about unusual bird species.

Organizations for Birders

American Birding Association
http://www.americanbirding.org/
This is a North American
organization whose aim is to inspire
people to enjoy and protect wild
birds.

American Society for the Protection of Nature in Israel
http://www.aspni.org/
ASPNI is a U.S. organization that
raises awareness and support for
the work of the Society for the
Protection of Nature in Israel. Its
director works very closely with
Yossi Leshem.

BirdLife International
http://www.birdlife.org/
BirdLife International is an
international partnership of
conservation organizations working
together to conserve birds and
protect their habitats.

British Trust for Ornithology
http://www.bto.org/
This British organization conducts
bird surveys and promotes
bird conservation through its
membership.

National Audubon Society
http://www.audubon.org/
The National Audubon Society is
a U.S. organization whose mission
is to conserve and restore natural
ecosystems. Its focus is on birds and
other wildlife.

Palestine Wildlife Society
http://www.wildlife-pal.org/
The Palestine Wildlife Society is
trying to build awareness of the
environment and the need for
conservation in the Palestinian
territories. The website showcases
the society's activities and projects.

Royal Society for the Conservation of Nature
http://www.rscn.org.jo
This website shows how the Royal
Society for the Conservation of
Nature in Jordan is balancing the
needs of the environment with the
needs of the local people.

Royal Society for the Protection of Birds
http://www.rspb.org.uk/
Britain's Royal Society for the
Protection of Birds bills itself
as "a million voices for nature."
The website tells about how this
organization works for the protection
of birds and the environment through
public awareness campaigns and the
operation of nature reserves.

INDEX

PHOTO ACKNOWLEDGMENTS

The following images were provided by Yossi Leshem: : Israeli Air Force, pp. 2 (all insets), 9, 36; Gilad Friedemann, p. 4; Yossi Eshbol, SPNI, pp. 5, 28; © Yossi Leshem, pp. 6 (inset), 7 (right), 26, 31, 32, 33, 37, 40, 48 (left), 49, 56, 58 (right, left anonymous), 59 (inset); Ryuichi Hirokawa, p. 10 (main); Martin Rinik, p. 14; Tuvia Kurtz, p. 24; Haim Alfiya, p. 30; Israeli Aircraft Industry, p. 34 (inset); Prof. Zvi Malik, p. 38; Motti Charter, pp. 43 (top), 50 (top); Gen. Baruch Shpiegel (Government Press Office), p. 43 (bottom); Dr. Leonid Dinevitch, p. 48 (right); Imad Atrash, p. 50 (bottom); SPNI, p. 52.

The following images are used with the permission of: © Eyal Bartov, pp. 1, 2 (main), 6 (main), 8, 20, 23, 25, 27, 41, 44 (left), 57, 59 (main), 61, 62; © blickwinkel/Alamy, p. 3; © Panda Photo/FLPA, p. 10 (inset); © Arthur Morris/Visuals Unlimited, pp. 11 (top), 17; AP Photo, p. 11 (bottom); REUTERS/Gary Hershorn, p. 13 (bottom); © Civil Aeuronautics Board, p. 13 (top); © Duby Tal/Albatross, p. 15; © Andy Rouse/The Image Bank/Getty Images, pp. 18 -19; © Charles Melton/Visuals Unlimited/Getty Images, p. 19 (inset); © Grant Faint/Photographer's Choice/Getty Images, p. 22; © Yossi Eshbol, pp. 29, 45; © age fotostock/SuperStock, p. 34 (main); © Lior Rubin, p. 39; © Amir Ezer, p. 42 (both); © Dr. Ofer Bahat, p. 44 (right); © Pierre Perin, pp. 46 (left), 60; © Benya Binnun, p. 46 (right); © Yoav Perlman, p. 47; © Dr. Michael Kaatz, p. 51; © Dubi Kalay, p. 53; © Yuval Assado, p. 54; © Barak Granit, p. 55.

Illustrations on pp. 12, 16, 17, 21, 24, 27, 35, 51 by © Laura Westlund/Independent Picture Service.

Cover: © Eyal Bartov.